Sanjeevani Bhelande

Meera & Me

Love Songs of Meerabai

Scan the QR codes and enjoy Sanjeevani's music on various streaming platforms:

Videos Audios

Sanjeevani Bhelande

Meera & Me

Love Songs of Meerabai

Foreword: Mahesh Bhatt

Popular Prakashan
www.popularprakashan.com

Dedicated
to my late Papa
whose pure spirit inspires me
at every step
and
to my spirited mother
for inculcating in me
the love of Truth, Perfection
and Wisdom

Published by
Harsha Bhatkal for
Popular Prakashan Pvt. Ltd.
301, Mahalaxmi Chambers
22, Bhulabhai Desai Road
Mumbai 400026
info@popularprakashan.com

First Published 2023

(4544)
ISBN: 978-81-956688-3-0

Creative Direction & Book Design: Nutan Asgaonkar ampersdesign.com

Devanagari calligraphy: Hemant Bharat Ravandale www.hrekmaadhyam.com

English translations editor: Dr Meenakshi Shivram, Dr Anjali Bhelande

Sanjeevani Photographs: Nitin Chitnis, Kunal Kaushal, Mandar Apte

Mahesh Bhatt Photograph courtesy: Krishnakant Bajpai

Cover Photograph: Mandar Apte

Photograph with Mahesh Bhatt: Ashray Goyal

Meera Mandir, Medta pictures: Mohan Mehriya

Illustrations: National merit award 2018 winning artiste Jitendra R Sharma

Nirmal Arts: Nirmal Sharma, Udaipur nirmalart2000@yahoo.com

Printed In India
by Saurabh Printers (P) Ltd.
Plot No. 67 A-68, Ecotech, Ext. I
Kasna, Greater Noida-201306 (U.P)

CONTENTS

1st January 2012

Sanjeevani's identification with Meera is phenomenal. Singing Meera, she transcends into Meera. I wonder, I should seek her blessings, or bless her for this spiritual effort!

(Gulzar)

"BOSKYANA", NARGIS DUTT ROAD, PALI HILL, BANDRA (WEST), MUMBAI - 400 050.

FOREWORD

In devotion, one has no choice. The wise believe that just as we are born with various organs, saints are born with devotion within them. Devotion is not something they acquire, but something that is part and parcel of their very DNA. Bhakt Meera discovered at the tender age of four the essence of devotion that lay deep within her being.

Meera was born a princess in Rajasthan, in 1498. One day, as Gokulashtami Utsav was being celebrated in her parental home, and sadhus sang devotional songs to the accompaniment of instruments like the *veena, mridangam* and cymbals, the heart of the four-year-old Meera was captivated by the passionate fervour that surrounded her. The pure essence of *Krishna Bhakti* (devotion to Lord Krishna) filled her heart and soul. She was never the same again.

Great sadhus who have trodden the path of devotion categorise it into two types: *sadhana bhakti* and *prem bhakti*. *Sadhana bhakti* is practising the path of devotion as laid down in the scriptures; *prem bhakti* is the natural outburst of the purest form of unconditional, selfless love towards one's deity and, therefore, considered superior to *sadhana bhakti*. The devoted say that it is rare to come across *prem bhakt*s for they are the greatest of all. The attributes of these *bhakt*s (devotees) are that they have the tenderest of hearts which melt whenever they think of their Lord. Little wonder then that even in these godless times, Meera, a personification of devotion, and her narrative, still continue to intoxicate people.

One such *bhakt* of the 21st century, right in the heart of the film business, where machines today do the work of minds, is Sanjeevani. With her tinkling voice and gentle demeanour, she carries about her the fragrance of India, having discovered a unique mantra to happiness in Meera's *'magan bhaav'* (an inward blissful state of being), and *'prem bhaav'* (state of being, overflowing with love). Sanjeevani singing *"Mere to Giridhar Gopal,"* transports us from the cacophony of today's world to another century where we may lose ourselves, possibly forever. Mercenaries in the music business wonder what compels a talent like Sanjeevani to immerse herself so completely in this extraordinary task of 'songslation' of Meera's *bhajans* (devotional songs), when she could have put that time to better use — singing songs to numb and not to inspire, and awaken.

To such people I would say that the world never comprehended Bhakt Meera in her times. Even the scriptures did not truly recognise or give cognisance to her independent spirit. But Meera did not care for all that. She cared only for the passion that she had for Lord Krishna. Likewise, Sanjeevani too, cares only for the music of Meera, which has been sourced from the heart of India.

Tales of unmatched devotion leave you awestruck. The devotion of little Prahlad towards Lord Hari transformed all the tortures meted out to him, into joyful experiences. Nothing is impossible when one is so devoted to one's god or icon? Devotion turns earth into water, fire into snow and poison into nectar! But only a devoted heart can truly understand this.

Despite the hostile environment into which Meera was born, she remained steadfast in her devotion to Krishna, and through that, became immortal. The world forces you to conform to its ways, but the brave dare to defy and to walk alone. The *bhakt*s say that while ordinary people quest after food, clothing and material wealth, and conform to the world's ways, the *bhakt* willingly immerses himself into the eternal ocean of love, flowing since the dawn of time.

Like Meera took birth for Krishna, lived for Krishna and finally, in her death, merged with Krishna, Sanjeevani was born to drown in Meera, and in a sense, immortalise her.

Meera may have been reduced to ashes, possibly scattered in the deserts of Rajasthan, but her spirit lives in the songs that Sanjeevani sings, in the sweet richness of her voice. Come, breathe deeply and experience the sheer beauty and elation that true devotion can bring.

Mahesh Bhatt

MEERA, A WOMAN OF ALL TIMES

Sanjeevani is known to me as 'Chhoti' — the little girl. With a name like that, there was no way we were ever going to let her grow — either up or in any other direction. And when she embarked on this Meera journey a few years ago and discovered many parallels between Meera's life and her own, there was no point absolutely in letting the 'Chhoti' appellation stay on.

Sanjeevani always wished only to sing. Like Meera, who did not see why she had to marry when she was already wedded to her Lord, Sanjeevani too did not see why she had to seek any other goal in life when she already had one. But she had to conform. She had to needlessly juggle mathematics with music. And one day, the cocoon had to burst open — the butterfly had to be born. Like Meera's magical *bhakti,* Sanjeevani's single-minded *sadhana* (quest) gently silenced her critics.

It would be simplifying the issue to casually state that every woman is like Meera or that there is a Meera lodged in every woman's heart. Nothing could be further from the truth. If gender divide is still a relevant issue in our world, it is because we do not have enough of the Meera-variety of feminists with us. Meera did not fight against or resist patriarchal control; she did not conveniently move away from the centre to seek her refuge in peripheral corners reserved for victims — she gently confronted all her critics and converted, not silenced, many of them. There are some battles you lose even when you win, and so they have to be strategised differently.

What is an editor's task when the master is so talented? I have added a word here, taken a word off there, changed a line here and added a rhyme there. And while the conservative in me wonders how Meera can call her lover "dude" or "boss", I have learnt, happily, that nothing brings you closer to *bhakti* than a rule-breaking spunk of irreverence. I have loved the phrase — "Jingles jangled" and the "Brazen Cowboy Blue".

I had serious doubts when I first encountered an English Meera — in getting the guitar and the sitar together, would we lose the mood of surrender? In changing Giridhar to "Mountain Man", were we replacing fondness with distance? How was this 'songslation' different from a re-mix? And finally, would the Meera of today nonchalantly say — *"Mere to Giridhar aur Gopal, teesro na koi"* (Mine are both Giridhar and Gopal, no other third one)? The answers were slow in the coming — Meera needs to be appropriated and owned by every generation of seekers; *Meera & Me* is not about the "Mountain Man" — it is about a very contemporary Meera who is ready once again to sing her way through the foolish expectations of the world; and, no, this is not a re-mix. There are the mainstream versions of Meera's *bhajans* sung by Lata Mangeshkar, Vani Jayram, Anup Jalota and M.S. Subbulakshmi that thrive along with many subaltern versions. Sanjeevani's collection is yet another version. And in true Advaitic spirit, the lover and the loved have to be One; there can be no *"doosro"* (second one) or *"teesro"* (third one).

Any work on Meera will always have to be a work-in-progress. Many of the songs in this collection have been set to music. But these are not final compositions. Who knows, the guitar strings might someday strum a new word and challenge this 'songslation', and who knows, one day Meera might wish to go Chinese. If Meera has chosen to speak to every generation, then to this generation she speaks as 'Sanjeera'.

My love to Chhoti — for embarking on this courageous and lonely journey, for gently dismantling all conservative positions of Meera-ownership, and for becoming the 'Badi' that she always was.

Dr. Meenakshi Shivram
Visiting Faculty (English) & Research Guide (S.N.D.T. University, Mumbai)
Sahitya Akademi Award winner for translation, 1998

MEET MY MEERA

"I am soul, not body. I'm a natural emotion, not a social norm" *(Main atman hun, shareer nahi; main bhavna hun, kisi samaj ka vichar nahi)*: these lines from Gulzar's screenplay of his film *Meera* (1978), triggered my journey to discovering mystical Meerabai.

I grew up singing popular Meera songs like *Payoji Maine Ram Ratan, Santo karam ki gat nyari, Chala vahi des* etc. These etched Meera's image on my mind: that of a pristine, passionate woman in love. The beauty, depth, simplicity and musical quality of her poetry mesmerised me. I spontaneously connected to her feminine longing for love, as well as her uninhibited self-expression. I discovered a unique magic mantra to happiness in Meera's 'magan bhaav' (an inward, blissful state of being), anand bhaav (joyous state) and 'prem bhaav' (state of being, overflowing with love). Every time I sang *"Payoji maine Ram rattan dhan payo"* (A radiant ruby is my find), I would be filled with joy and would easily lose myself in Meera's world.

The word 'Meera' means 'ocean' or 'oasis' in Sanskrit and I yearned to take this oasis of love to the world. Was I qualified to take up the huge task of interpreting Meera's profound love for her Lord, expressed in such lyrical brilliance? Following my heart's call, I plunged into the Meera ocean in the belief that Meera would show me the way. Just as Meera surrendered to her mystic man: "Divine love is a novel road, the precious path, pray show" *(Prem bhakti ro panth hee nyaro, humko gayl bataaja)*, I too surrendered myself to this saint-poet. And Meera unwittingly became my friend, guide and inspiration.

Meera, the princess

Born a princess in 1498 in Medta, Rajasthan, Meera has been described as a very beautiful woman full of poise and grace, one with artistic and philosophical leanings. She was married into the royal family of Chittoud as part of a political alliance. But, Meera believed herself to be married to her Lord Krishna. She sang songs in His praise and danced in ecstasy, oblivious of the norms of propriety and decorum of her times and class. She left the luxuries of palace life, abandoned the social role of a married woman and embraced the simple life of a seeker.

Meera, the woman

The strength and self-assurance with which Meera lived her life is inspiring. She simply followed the dictates of her heart. Her innermost promptings elevated her from the gross to the subtle, the mundane to the sublime, and the human to the divine. It was her feminine capacity that enabled her to abandon herself to an 'other-centered love'. Using the metaphor of human love, Meera's spirituality is unveiled gradually:

"At midnight O Master, come by the river, Meera's heart is more than eager to meet her melodious lover'' *(Aadha raat Prabhu darsan deejyo jamnajee re teera, Meera re Prabhu Giridhar Nagar, hivro ghano adheera)*.

"A veil of five senses I wore, I played a game of peek-a-boo" *(Panchrang chola pehenya sakhi, jharmat khelan jati)*.

Although Meera was a beautiful woman, who defied societal norms and stepped out of the mould of marriage, she is revered and loved throughout India even today. Somewhere down the line, the gender identification fades and it becomes irrelevant that Meera was a woman.

I feel there is a Meera in every woman who strives for excellence and perfection, thereby forging an identity beyond her womanhood.

"When Mahatma Gandhi chose Meera as an inspirational figure for a modern Indian renaissance, he was showing his unerring instinct for the right symbol,'' observed aptly novelist and translator, Shama Futehally.

Meera, the mystic

In medieval India, women had restricted access to spirituality beyond the confines of their homes. Meera once sought the blessings of a revered Hindu priest at Brindavan. The priest refused to meet her because she was a woman. Meera argued that the only man is the Lord himself. The rest are devotees, and the soul has no gender. "Meera pointed out the femininity of the true devotee who loves the Lord like a woman. She uses 'man' as a metaphor for the One who has the real power. Most devotees like Meera, ultimately come to a realisation of the truth of Oneness, that the lover and the beloved are not separate after all," says Swati Chopra.

Intelligent life energy is beyond gender. It is a predominant Hindu belief that the soul *(atma),* after death merges with the larger consciousness *(parmatma).* In the *Samkhya* philosophy, there is *Purush* (Supreme Consciousness) and *Prakriti* (the created world) — the *essence* and its *manifestation.* At the end of the quest, individual consciousness merges with Supreme Consciousness. Meera could see beyond the popular notions of a limited being. She lived on a different dimension, identifying herself with a subtle pulsating energy. She refused to get caught up in the superficial and the gross. Her enlightenment is simple: discovery of a special 'wealth' more valuable than all the life-long accumulation of material things. "Spend yet gain, thugs loot in vain. Day by day, the wealth multiplies. A radiant ruby is my find" *(Kharch na khoote, chor na loote, din din badhat savaayo. Payoji maine Ramratan dhan payo).*

Meera's poems are an expression of her philosophy: faith and detachment. "Once detached, there's no wrong, ever immersed in my inner song; Meera says, in life's ping-pong, come what may, go along" *(Karna fakiri, phir kya dilgiri, sada magan mai rehena ji; Meera kahe Prabhu Giridhar Nagar, aaye pade so sehna ji).* This is not the careless abandon of the irresponsible, but the carefree expansion of a limitless soul.

"Meera faced persecution but she neither struggled nor suffered heroically. She simply found it irrelevant," writes Shama Futehally.

"Equanimity," writes Dr. Anjali Bhelande in *Self, Beyond Self,* "is the great ideal that the *Gita* is never tired of emphasising. Subjective equanimity implies sameness in joy and sorrow, honour and dishonour and in all situations of life. Objective equanimity implies regarding all people with equal eyes regardless of whether someone is good or evil, friend or foe. The final stage of equanimity is when one is absolutely unperturbed by worldly things. In fact, one goes beyond them and becomes one with the Universal Soul."As modern day spiritual Master Rajiv Kapur puts it, "Be like the calm ocean bed, unaffected by the turbulent surface waves." This is the spirit of equanimity that Meera exhibits in her songs. *"Samta tol dharungi ho"* (Calm and content within, I will hold my balance).

Several Meera fans have commented on her ability to easily fuse the human and the spiritual.

Robert Bly feels, "Meerabai's experience is as recognisably grounded in a fully human passion as it is in the realm of spiritual realisation.''

In Gulzar's screenplay of his film on Meera, Guru Sant Raidas comments that his follower Meera had the spiritual yearning of an ascetic as well as the joyous passion of a young bride *(Bairaginonka dard aur suhaginonka ka russ hain Meera mein).*

According to Andrew Schelling, "Meera asserted her demand for artistic, spiritual and sexual freedom."

'Songslation', not translation

Meera is loved, among other things, for the sheer 'singability' of her poems. The original language which has a lilting, lyrical vocabulary is a combination of Rajasthani, Gujarati and a medieval Hindi dialect called Brij. The "delicate filigree of sound" as Shama Futehally describes it, the simple, lucid style filled with alliteration and onomatopoeia, the flawless metre and the spontaneous rhyme scheme — how could all this be rendered in another language? The cadences and prosody of an Indian song are tough to translate into the English language. Meera's poems are even more difficult as they are a heady combination of words, tune and mood.

To preserve the musical quality of Meera's lyrics, I have consciously made a generous use of rhyme and musical sounding alliteration. I tried to find apt words that conveyed both Meera's intensity as well as the euphonious melody of her poetry. What we have is Meera's poems and not merely her songs in English. These can be set to music and sung. While rhymes are not a precondition for this, Meera's poems rhyme so effortlessly that they are intrinsically hummable. In what I call my 'songslation', I have sought to retain the musical flavour and have accordingly taken liberties with the English language. The 32 Meera poems that I have selected represent a variety of moods and themes.

The language

Meera's *mukt bhaav* (free spirit), *anand bhaav* (joyousness) and *prem bhaav* (love), have a universality and timelessness that transcend cultural and temporal boundaries. "Meera addressed Him in the most intimate terms, over-stepping all propriety," comments Robert Bly. Therefore, I adapted a contemporary style of expression in these songs.

I have consciously avoided the names Krishna or Giridhar Gopal, as I want readers of every faith to relate to Meera's predicament. This book is about Meera and not the Lord. I have translated her signature lines differently each time. *"Meera ke Prabhu Giridhar Nagar"* becomes, in my renditions, "Meera met her Mountain Man" or "Meera's is the Mighty Milkman'', "He who held the hill high", etc.

Words like "honey", "my guy", "my boss" *(saheb)*, "baby", etc., lend a bright, bold dimension, and Meera was bold.

Some Indian words are now part of the English language, for instance, guru, yoga, chukar (chakor), Om, sari, sanyasi. Hence I have retained some of these.

Cultural allusions

Certain references in Meera's poems have to be understood within a specific cultural context:

- *'Ghunghru'* is different from anklet *(payal)*, being an ornament with a 100 tiny bells used by classical dancers. Hence *'pug ghunghroo'* became "Jingles tied to her feet, Meera danced to the beat."
- *'Bairaag'* or renunciation is used in a very different sense by Meera. She renounced the world in search of her love. Her's is not the austere detachment of a hermit. She gave up this world only to seek another for her love. Her renunciation was such that she lived in a continuous state of ecstasy. "I'll drape the very yarn spun, that pleases my Dark One. Babes, I'll be a nun, Oh yeah" *(Ji ji bhes mhara saheb rijhe, soi bhes dharoongi ho. Bala main bairagan hui ho)*.
- *'Janam-janam'* distills the concept of rebirth, a part of Hinduism. It is believed that one is born in the human form only once in eighty-four lakh births. Meera refers to her love that must have had its origins in previous lives and carries on for several births. For example, "You gave your word in past lives" or "the virgin waits life after life", etc. There are also references to the concept of *'moksh'* (liberation from the cycle of birth-death-rebirth), that consolidate the idea of a relationship not limited to this birth alone.

"To her Lord, Meera belongs, free me of rebirth, Almighty Boss" *(Meera re Prabhu Giridhar Nagar, aavagaman nivaar)*. Hence Kumkum Sangari rightly concludes: "Meera chooses an immortal bridegroom and gains *achal suhaag* (eternal matrimonial bliss)."

- *'Saavan'* or the monsoon season in India, has been seen for centuries by poets as the season of romance. To a person in London, a rainy day may be a dull, yet-another-umbrella-day. But for Meera, the rains symbolise a breaking open of the skies that comes as deliverance to the parched lands. "Clouds shower monsoon bliss, what a romantic season is this! My heart dances in the rain, as I sense His presence again" *(Barse badariya saavanki, saavan ki manbhaavan ki; Saavan mein umangyo mero mann, bhanak suni Hari aawan ki)*.
- Holi is an Indian festival of colours celebrated across the northern and western parts of India, to mark the onset of spring. It is believed that Lord Krishna played Holi smearing everyone with a red powder called *gulal*. Holi signifies fun, cheer and romance. Meera, however, finds Holi colourless without her beloved.

Meera and me again

Meera has become my passion, my mission. In her, I discovered a modern liberated woman, the Lady of Liberty, a free spirit. I have tried to explore Meera's universality so that my Indian friends overseas too can take Meera to their children and help them understand their multi-cultural identity. To take Meera's music to the world, I have recorded an album of these songs in a unique format fusing the Hindi words with the English lyrics, drums with the *duff* (hand-held percussion instrument), and the guitar with the sitar.

When Meera says, "Pearls, corals I showed the door, a garland of wild flowers I wore" *(Moti moonge utaar, Banmala poi)*, I see a woman dropping the crutch of external ornaments, shining with her inner beauty. I admire Meera's uncompromising attitude. Human love is transient and selfish. She would settle for nothing less than the purest of the pure — Divine Love! I am awestruck by her ability to love so perfectly, so completely. Meera lost her mother at an early age, her husband soon after her marriage and, later, her father. Osho has so rightly said: "Meera realised that everything in this universe is momentary. If the beloved is to be sought, seek in the Eternal."

"To sing and pray is the happy way" *(Gunn ganwa sukh paasya)* sums up the simple soul that is Meera. I sing all the time. I sing when I cook, when I water the plants, when I'm in the shower, during walks, in the studio and on stage. I know exactly what Meera means. To sing is indeed the happy way.

Once you are touched by the Meera magic, you are smitten for life. To read Meera is to awaken deeply in your own life. Words can hardly capture Meera's luminous presence. *Meera & Me*, in line with Meera's samarpann bhaav (sense of surrender), is a humble tribute to her blazing spirit.

I feel blessed to present the second, revised edition of my book *Meera & Me*. The added feature is the QR codes that are linked to the YouTube videos of my songs. Thank you Harsha Bhatkal for this suggestion and for joining hands in my Meera mission.

Sanjeevani Bhelande

Sanjeevani at Meera's birth place, Medta, in Rajasthan (pp. 23-25).

मीरा के श्याम

Radiant Ruby

पायोजी मैंने रामरतन धन पायो

वस्तु अमोलिक दी म्हारे सतगुरु
किरपा कर अपनायो

जनमजनम की पूंजी पाई
जगमें सभी खोवायो

खर्च ना खूटे चोर ना लूटे
दिनदिन बढ़त सवायो

सत् की नाव खेवटिया सतगुरु
भवसागर तरि आयो

मीरा के प्रभु गिरिधर नागर
हरख हरख जस गायो

A radiant ruby is my find.

He blessed me with a gem divine,
And took me in His care so kind.

An age-old treasure is mine,
For worldly pleasures left behind.

Spend yet gain, thugs loot in vain,
Day by day, the wealth multiplies.

Truth my ferry, He my guide,
Through life's ocean I glide.

He who held the hill high,
'Hail Him,' Meera sings overjoyed.

Scan Qr Code
For Video

The Dream Song

माई म्हाणो सुपणामां
परण्यां रे दिनानाथ

छप्पण कोटां जणां पधार्‍या
दूल्हो श्री बृजनाथ

सुपणामां तोरण बंध्या रे
सुपणामां गह्या हाथ

सुपणामां म्हाणे परण गया
पाया अचल सुहाग

मीरा रो गिरीधर मिल्या रे
पूरब जणम रो भाग

Ma He wed me,
In my dream.

Fifty six-crore people teemed,
To bless the Groom Supreme.

He took my hand in the dream,
Under the floral beam.

He wed me in the dream,
I gained this timeless status esteemed.

Meera met her Mountain Man,
Past deeds are redeemed.

Meera Danced

पग घुंगरु बांध
मीरा नाची रे

मैं तो अपने नारायणकी
आपही हो गई दासी रे
लोग कहे मीरा भई बांवरी
सासू कहे कुलनासी रे

विष रो प्यालो राणा भेज्यो
पीवा मीरा हांसी रे
तणमण वार्या हरी चरणा माँ
थारी सरणा आस्यां रे

मीरा के प्रभु गिरिधर नागर
दरसन अमृत प्यासी रे

Jingles tied to her feet,
Meera danced to the beat.

I willingly made,
Myself His maid.
Folks said, Meera's gone mad,
She stabbed the family line elite.

The king sent a cup of poison,
Meera drank with a smile.
Soul and skin She surrendered,
At His feet, she went to meet.

Meera's Lord is the mountain man,
She thirsts for His glimpse sweet.

Scan Qr Code
For Video

The Rain Song

बरसे बदरियां सावनकी
सावन की मनभावन की

सावन में उमंग्यो मेरो मन
भनक सुनी हरी आवनकी

उमड़घुमड़ घन मेघां आयां
दामिनी घन झर ळावनकी
बीज्या बूंदा मेहा आयां
सीतळ पवन सुहावन री

मीरा के प्रभु गिरीधर नागर
बेळा मंगळ गावन की

Clouds shower monsoon bliss,
What a romantic season is this!

My heart dances in the rain,
As I sense His presence again.

Thunder and lightning,
Roar and flash,
The breeze is so cooling,
Raindrops splash.

The rains bring Meera's King.
It's time to welcome, time to sing.

Scan Qr Code
For Video

Break-Off Song

जो तुम तोड़ो पिया
मैं नाही तोड़ूं रे
तोसो प्रीत तोड़ क्रिष्णा
कौन संग जोड़ुं रे

तुम भये तरुवर
मैं भई पंखिया
तुम भये सरोवर
मैं तेरी मछिया

तुम भये गिरीवर
मैं भई चारा
तुम भये चंदा
मैं भई चकोरा

तुम भये मोती प्रभुजी
हम भये धागा
तुम भये सोना
हम भये सुहागा

मीरा कहे प्रभु
ब्रिजके वासी
तुम मेरे ठाकुर
मैं तेरी दासी

Even if, you break off,
Honey, I will not.
If I were to break off,
I won't tie the knot.

If You were a tree,
I'd be a birdie,
If You were the sea,
A fish I would be.

If You were the mountain,
I'd take shelter,
If You were the moon,
I'd thirst like a chukar.

If You were a pearl, Lord,
I'd be the string,
If You were gold,
It's sheen i would bring.

Says Meera,
O Brij resident,
You are my Master,
I'm Your servant.

Scan Qr Code
For Video

Ferry Me Across

म्हारो बेड़ो लगाज्यो पार
प्रभुजी अरज करूं छूं

या भवमां म्हे बहु दुख पायो
सांसा सोग निवार

अष्ट करमकी तलब लगी है
दूर करो दुखभार

यो संसार सब बह्यो जात है
लाख चौरासी धार

मीरां रे प्रभु गिरिधर नागर
आवागमन निवार

Ferry me across,
O Lord I humbly ask.

In this world, sorrow I grossed,
Free my breath of such dross.

I crave for the eight-fold path,
Ease the burden of my cross.

In rills, one lakh eighty-four,
The river of life, ceaselessly flows.

To her Lord, Meera belongs,
Free me of rebirth, Almighty Boss.

The Inner Song

करना फकिरी फिर क्या दिलगीरी
सदा मगन मैं रहना जी

कोई दिन गाड़ी न कोई दिन बंगला
कोई दिन जंगल रहना जी

कोई दिन हाथी न कोई दिन घोड़ा
कोई दिन पैदल चलना जी

कोई दिन चटाई कोई दिन दोलिया
कोई दिन भुई पर लेटना जी

मीरा कहे प्रभु गिरीधर नागर
आए पड़े सो सहना जी

Once detached, there's no wrong,
Ever immersed in my inner song.

At times a castle, at times a car,
At times in the jungle you slog.

At times you ride an elephant or horse,
At times on foot you walk for long.

At times cushions, at times a mat,
At times to the floor you belong.

Meera says, in life's ping-pong,
Come what may, go along.

Scan Qr Code
For Video

To His House I Go

मैं तो गिरीधर के घर जाऊँ

To His house I go.

गिरीधर म्हारो सांचो प्रीतम
देखत रूप लुभाऊँ

He's my true beau,
His looks my mind blow.

रैन पड़े तब ही उठी जाऊँ
भोर भये उठी आऊँ

I step out when dark,
At dawn, back I tiptoe.

रैन दिन वाके संग खेलू
ज्यो त्यो वाही रिझाऊँ

Night and day with Him I play,
To please and pamper Him so.

जो पहरावे सोई पहरु
जो दे सोई खाऊँ

His choice is mine,
In food and clothes.

म्हारी उनकी प्रीत पुरानी
उन बिन पल ना रहाऊँ

Our love is ages old,
Can't bear a moment alone.

जहाँ बैठावे तिथी बैठू
बेचे तो बिक जाऊँ

I gladly sit where told.
If He sells me, am sold.

मीरा रे प्रभु गिरीधर नागर
बारबार बलि जाऊँ

O Meera's Mighty Muse,
Over and over, I love You more.

Dyed Deep Blue

म्हां गिरिधर रंग राती

पंचरंग चोला पेहर्‍यां सखी
झरमट खेलन जाती

वा झरमटमां मिल्या साँवरो
देख्या तनमन राती

जिनरो पिया परदेस बस्यारी
लिखलिख भेज्यां पाती

म्हारा पिया म्हारे हिवड़ा बसता
ना आवां ना जाती

मीरा रे प्रभु गिरिधर नागर
मग जोवां दिन राती

I dyed myself a deep deep blue.

A veil of five senses I wore,
I played a game of peek-a-boo.

Seeing Him I dropped my veil,
I gave my body and soul too.

Those whose lovers are far away,
Are sent letters, day after day.

My lover is etched Deep in my heart.
No coming, no going, He bonds like glue.

Day and night Meera awaits,
Her Lord who lifted the hill in rescue.

Scan Qr Code
For Video

The Brazen Cowboy Blue

मेरे तो गिरिधर गोपाल
दूसरो न कोई

जाके सर मोर मुकूट
मेरो पति सोई

तातमात बंधुभ्रात
आपणो ना कोई

छांड दई कुलकी कानी कहा करिये कोई
संतन ढिग बैठीबैठी लोक लाज खोई

चुनरी के लिये टूक
ओढ़ लीनी लोई

मोती मूँगे उतार
बनमाला पोई

आंसुवन जल सींचीसींची प्रेम बेल बोई
अब तो बेल फैल गई आनंद फल होई

दूधकी मथनियाँ बड़े प्रेमसे बिलोई
माखन जब काढ़ लियो छाछ पिये कोई ?

भगति देख राजी हुई
जगत देख रोई

दासी मीरां लाल गिरिधर
तारो अब मोई

Mine is the Brazen Blue Cowboy,
And no one else.

Only the peacock crowned,
Is my man.

My mom, my dad, my brother,
Ain't no kin.

Some claim, I crushed the family name.
Befriending the saints, I quit shame.

I tore my silk scarf to shreds,
With a simple stole, I covered my head.

Pearls, corals I showed the door,
A garland of wild flowers I wore.

My tears watered a love seed sown,
The tree's now grown, joy fruits it has borne.

The milk I fondly churned away,
The cream once taken, who wants whey?

Faith brings joy,
The world makes me cry.

Meera's your maid, O Mountain-boy.
In life, be my buoy.

Scan Qr Code
For Video

J.R. SHARMA

I Bought The Lord

माई री
मैं तो लियो गोविन्द मोल

कोई कहे छाने
कोई कहे चुपके
लियो री बजन्ता ढोल

कोई कहे मोंघो
मैं कहा सस्तो
लियो री तराजू मोल

कोई कहे कारो
कोई कहे गोरो
आवो री प्रेमके मोल

तन वारा म्हां जीवन वारा
वारा अमोलक मोल

मीरा के प्रभु दरसन दीजो
पूरब जणम रो कौल

Hey Mom,
I've bought the Lord.

Some say, 'It's on the sly,'
Some pass comments wry,
Beating drums Him I did buy.

'That's steep,' some say,
'It's cheap,' I say,
On scales, His worth I did weigh.

'He's dark,' some declare,
Some said, 'He's very fair,'
I got Him for love and care.

My body and life I'll sacrifice,
I've paid a priceless price.

Give me a glimpse, Meera prays,
You promised so, in bygone days.

Scan Qr Code
For Video

The Happy Way

माई म्हां गोविन्द गुण गास्यां

चरणामृत रो णेम सकारे
नित उठ दरसन जास्यां

हरी मंदिर मां नृत्य करावा
घूँघरिया घमकास्यां

श्याम नाम रो झांझ चलास्यां
भोसागर तर जास्यां

यो संसार बीड़ रो कांटो
घेल प्रीत अटकास्यां

मीरा रे प्रभु गिरीधर नागर
गुण गावां सुख पास्यां

God's glory I sing away.

To touch His feet,
I'm up everyday.

Wearing jingles, in His temple,
I dance and sway.

Clanging cymbals in His name,
I sail through life's ocean bay.

The world hurts like a thorn,
Stuck in love's lane forlorn.

Meera's Lord is a classy guy,
To sing and pray is the happy way.

The Home-Coming

म्हारो ओळगिया घर आया जी

तनकी ताप मिटी सुख पाया
हिळमिळ मंगळ गाया जी

घन की धुन सुन मोर मगन भया
म्हारे आंगण आंज्यो जी

चंदा देख कमोदन फूलां
हरख भया म्हारी काया जी

रोमरोम म्हारो सीतळ सजनी
मोहन महळ सिधार्यो जी

सब भगतन रा कारज साधा
म्हारा परण निभाज्यो जी

मीरा बिरहन गिरिधर नागर
मिळ दुख दुंदा नास्यां जी

My Beloved has come home, my dear.

Gone is my ache, happy is my state,
I'll sing songs of good cheer.

The peacock dances to the thunder beat,
Come into my home-sphere.

On seeing the moon, the lotus blooms,
On my skin, goose-bumps appear.

Every pore feels cool to the core,
Look girls, my Lord is here.

Dreams of devotees, You made come true,
Grant me my wish sincere.

Meeting her Mountain Man,
Makes Meera's pain disappear.

Honour My Love

सांवरो म्हारी प्रीत निभाज्यो जी

थें छो म्हारो गुण रो सागर
अवगुण म्हां बिसराज्यो जी

लोक ना सीझ्यां, मन ना पतीज्यां
मुखड़ा सबद सुणाज्यो जी

दासी थांरी जणमजणम री
म्हारो आंगण आंज्यो जी

मीरा रे प्रभु गिरिधर नागर
बेड़ा पार लगाज्यो जी

Honour my love, O Lord Dusky Grey.

You are my ocean of virtue,
Forgive my flaws, I pray.

The world may mock, my faith is like rock,
One word from Your lips, do say.

I'm Your maid, life after life,
Come, O come to my doorway.

Meera's Lord has a refined way,
Tide me through each day.

Brindavan

आळी म्हाने लागा बृंदावनणीका

घरघर तुळसी ठाकर पूजा
दरसन गोविंदजीका

निर्मळ नीर बहया जमुनामां
भोजन दूध दहयाका

रतन सिंघासन आप बिराज्या
मुगट धर्‍यां तुळसीका

कुंजनकुंजन फिर्‍यां साँवरा
सबद सुन्या मुरळीका

मीरा के प्रभु गिरधर नागर
भजन बिना नर फीका

Sis, I love Brindavan's feel.

To worship Him and the Tulsi tree,
In every home they bow and kneel.

The Yamuna flows on, crystal clean,
Milk and curd are a daily meal.

He sits on a throne of gems real,
His leafy crown is of Basil.

His flute fills the garden green,
My Beloved Blue, it reveals.

*O Meera's Lord with the wheel,**
Minus His song, life is an ordeal.

I'll Be A Nun

बाला मैं बैरागन हुई हो

जीजी भेस म्हारा साहेब रीझे
सोई भेस धरुंगी हो

सीलसंतोष धरुं घट भीतर
समता पकड़ रखूंगी हो

जाको नाम निरंजन कहिये
ताको ध्यान धरुंगी हो

गुरु ग्यान रंगू तन कपड़ा
मन मुद्रा फेरुंगी हो

प्रेम प्रीतसू हरि गुन गाऊँ
चरनन लिपट रहूंगी हो

या तन की मैं करु किंगारी
रसना राम रटूंगी हो

मीरा के प्रभु गिरीधर नागर
साधा संग रहूंगी हो

Oh Baby, I'll be a nun!

I'll wear the very clothes spun,
That please my Dark One!

Calm, content, within I'll keep,
Equanimity in my conscience.

His name's my aim,
All other thoughts I'll shun.

My Guru moulds my mind,
I'll soak my skin in his sapience.

I'll hum His hymns and hug
His feet with affection.

I'll make my body a banjo,
His song on it I will run.

Meera reveres the mountain man,
Without His hymn, there's no fun!

Love-Crazy

एरी मैं तो प्रेम दिवानी
मेरो दर्द ना जाने कोई

घायल की गत घायल जाने
और ना जाने कोई

जौहर कीमत जौहर जाने
की जिन जौहरी होई

सूली उपर सेज हमारी
सोवन किस बिध होई

गगन मंड़लपर सेज पियाकी
किस बिध मिलना होई

दर्द की मारी बन बन फिरु
बैद मिल्या नही कोई

मीरा के प्रभु पीड़ मिटे जब
बैद सांवरिया होई

Oh Honey, I'm love-crazy,
Oh my pain Nobody knows.

The one who bleeds knows,
The pangs of the blows.

It's in the jeweller's hands,
That the gem really glows.

My bed hangs on a cross,
How do I sleep-pose.

My lover's bed is up in the sky,
Will we ever come close?

No cure for my pain,
I roam the wilds on my toes.

Meera's doc is her Lord,
He alone can heal her woes.

Scan Qr Code
For Video

Take A Bow!

म्हारो प्रणाम बांके बिहारी जी

मोर मुगट माथे
तिलक बिराज्यां
कुंडल अलकां करी जी

अधर मधुर धर
बन्सी बजावां
रीझ रिझावां बृज नारी जी

या छब देख्यां मोह्यां मीरा
मोहन गिरिवर धारी जी

Take a bow my Majestic Master!

Peacock crown and a dot red,
He wears on His forehead,
Ear-rings of gold, glow and glitter.

His lips on the flute,
Play a magical tune.
Spellbound, the women of Brij appear.

Meera is sold out on the Charmer,
Who held the mountain on His finger.

Mud-Slinging

राणोजी
म्हाणे या बदनामी ळागे मीठी

कोई निंदो कोई बिंदो
मैं चळूँगी चाळ अनूठी

सांकडळी सेरिया सतगुरु मिलिया
क्यों कर फिरुं अपूठी

सतसंगतीमां ग्यान सुणेछी
दुर्जन ळोगां नेई दीठी

मीरां रे प्रभु गिरिधर नागर
दुर्जन जळो जा अंगीठी

I savour O King,
This mud-slinging.

Some approve, some disapprove,
I'll do my own thing.

In a slim street, I met my mentor,
Why would I go a-wandering?

I sat soaking in saintly sapience,
And ignored the evil beings.

Meera's Lord lifted the hill,
Mean men can go burn in the kiln.

So Much To Tell You

थाणे कांई कांई बोळ सुणावां
म्हारा साँवरा गिरिधारी

पूरब जणमरी प्रीती पुराणी
जावा णा गिरिधारी

सुंदर वदण जोवना साजण
थारी छबि बळिहारी

म्हारे आंगण स्याम पधारां
मंगळ गावां नारी

मोती चौक पुरावां नैणा
तन मन ड़ारां वारी

चरण सरणरी दासी मीरा री
जणमजणम री क्वांरी

So much to tell You, so much to say,
O my Dark One, of the mountains grey.

I've loved You the ages through,
Don't ever go, I beg of You.

Your charming form when I behold,
I fall in love, times untold.

My Dusky One has come home,
Maidens chant the holy 'Om'.

Pearls pure, love sincere,
My eyes shower as You appear.

Meera's a virgin at His feet,
Life after life she waits to meet.

Scan Qr Code
For Video

Doused In His Hue

मैं तो साँवरे के रंग राँची

साजि सिंगार बाँध पग घुँगरू
लोकलाज तजि नाची

गई कुमति, लिया साधां संगत
भगत रूप भई साँची

गायां गायां हरी गुण निसदिन
काल ब्याल री बाँची

श्याम बिना जग खारां लागां
जग री बातां काँची

मीरा श्री गिरिधर नटनागर
भगति रसीली जाँची

I doused myself in His hue.

Dressed pretty neat, bells bound to feet,
I danced to the beat, shame I threw.

I shed bad traits and stayed with saints,
Like a devotee true.

I sang His song every day,
And bid bad times adieu.

Without my beau, the world's a bore,
Words seem a sham too.

Oh mighty Mountain Hero,
Meera believes only in You.

J.R. SHARMA

The Clouds Made Me Cry

बादळ देख झरी शाम मैं
बादळ देख झरी

काळा पीळा घटा उमड्यां
बरसो चार घड़ी

जित जोया तित पानीपानी
प्यासां भूम हरी

म्हारा पिया परदेस बसतां
भींज्या बाहर खड़ी

मीरा के प्रभु हरी अविनासी
करस्यो प्रीत खरी

I wept, O Blue Beloved,
The clouds made me cry.

Black and beige, they rumbled and rained,
Four hours went by.

Water, water all around,
The green earth is parched and dry.

My lover lives in lands afar,
I stood out soaking under the sky.

Meera's is the Lord Eternal,
True love, I seek in reply.

Brother-In-Law

राणाजी
थें क्यांने राखो म्हांसूं बैर

थें तो राणाजी म्हाने ईसड़ा लागो
ज्यों बृच्छन मां केर

महल अटारी हम सब त्यागे
त्याग्यो थारो बसणो सहर

काजळ टीकी राणा हम सब त्याग्या
भगवीं चादर पहर

मीरा रे प्रभु गिरिधर नागर
अमृत कर दियो जहर

Brother-in-law,
Why make me your foe?

O King, I'm lovelorn,
As if pricked by a bush thorn.

I left the palace dome,
And the city of my home.

O King, I quit, kohl and rouge.
I wore a saffron robe.

Meera's Lord is a magician,
Who made nectar out of poison.

I'm Off To His Land

चाला वाही देस,
प्रीतम पावा
चाला वाही देस

कहो कसुमल साड़ी रंगावा
कहो तो भगवा भेस

कहो तो मोतियन माँग भरावा
कहो तो छिटकावा केस

मीरा के प्रभु गिरिधर नागर
सुणज्यो बिड़द नरेस

I'm off to His land,
To be one with my Lover,
I'm off to His land.

I'll drape a sari bright and red,
Or wear a saffron robe bland.

I'll sprinkle pearls on my part,
Or chop my tresses short, if you demand.

Oh King, take heed,
Meera has given the Lord her hand.

Scan Qr Code
For Video

Root of Pain

जोगिया री प्रीत है दुखड़ारो मूल

हिलमिल बात बनावत मीठी
पीछे जावत भूल

तोड़त जेज करत नही सजनी
जैसे चमेली के फूल

मीरा कहे प्रभु तुम्हरे दरस बिन
लागत हिवड़ा में सूल

To love a saint is the root of pain.

He whispers sweet refrains,
Then forgets me again.

He plucks me promptly,
Like a fragrant flower, O friend.

Meera says, without You Lord,
A thorn hurts my heart's vein.

J.R.SHARMA

Don't Go

मत जा मत जा मत जा जोगी
पाँव पड़ू मैं तोरी चेरी हो

प्रेम भक्ती रो पंथही न्यारो
हमको गैळ बता जा

अगर चंदनकी चिता रचाऊँ
अपने हात जळा जा

जळजळ भई भस्मकी ढ़ेरी
अपने अंग ळगा जा

मीरा के प्रभु गिरीधर नागर
ज्योत से ज्योत मिळा जा

Don't go, please don't go,
O Mystic, I touch Your toes.

Divine love is a novel road,
The precious path, pray show.

I'll stack a sandalwood pyre,
With Your hands, set it afire.

I'll burn to a heap of ashes,
Rub them on Your body and soul.

O Meera's Lord of yore,
Flame on flame, fuse ever more.

Scan Qr Code
For Video

J.R.SHARMA

My Mountain Guy

म्हां गिरीधर आगां नाच्या री

नाच नाच म्हां रसिक रिझावां
प्रीत पुरातन जांच्यां री

श्याम प्रीतरो बांध घुँघरिया
मोहन म्हारो सांच्यां री

लोक लाज कुल रां मर्यादा
जगमें नेक ना राख्यां री

प्रीतम पलछिन ना बिसरावां
मीरा हरिरंग राच्यां री

I danced before my Mountain Guy.

Danced and danced to please His eye,
An ancient love to testify.

My anklets, His love signify,
On my True One, I fully rely.

Status, honour, royal rites,
One and all I chose to defy.

Not a moment I forget Him aye,
Meera's doused in His dye.

The Holi Song

होली पिया बिन लागा री खा

This day of Holi, I miss Him dearly.

सूनो गांव देस सब सूनो
सूनी सेज्ज अटारी
सूनी बिरहन पिव बिन उ
त्यज्ज गया पिव प्यारी
बिरहा दुखकी मारी

The town, the country, all look gloomy,
Gloomy seem my bed and balcony.
Her lover has left,
The girl is lonely,
The agony knocks her silly.

देस बिदेसा सणेसा न जावा
म्हारो अणेसा भारी
गणतागणता घिस गया रेख
आंगरिया री सारी
आया ना मुरारी

He is far, no mail, no message,
Time weighs heavily.
Over and over I count and tally,
My finger lines fade fully,
The flautist eludes daily.

बाज्यां झांझ मृदंग मुरलिया
बाज्यां करा इकतारी
आया बसंत पिया घर नारी
म्हारी पीड़ा भारी
स्याम मने क्यारी बिसारी

Drums, cymbals, flutes sing,
Lone drones a single string,
My lover is lost and it's spring,
I'm at despair's brink,
How could You forget me, Honey?

ठाड़ी अरज्ज करयां गिरीधारी
राख्यां लाज्ज हमारी
मीरा रे प्रभु मिलस्यो माधो
जणमज्जणमरी क्वांरी
मने लागी दरसन थारी

I urge You humbly,
Honour my plea,
I'm Your devotee,
O Meera's Lord, come meet me.
This virgin waits endlessly.

Scan Qr Code
For Video

Make Me Your Maid

म्हाने चाकर राखां जी
गिरीधारी लाल चाकर राखां जी

चाकर रहस्यूँ बाग लगास्यूँ
नित उठ दरसन पास्यूँ
बृंदावन री कुंज गैलमां
गोविन्द लीला गास्यूँ

चाकरीमां दरसन पास्यूँ
सुमिरन पास्यूँ खरची
भाव भगत जागीरां पास्यूँ
जणमजणम री तरसी

मोर मुगुट पीताम्बर सोहां
गल बैजंता माळो
बृंदावनमां धेन चरावां
मोहन मुरलीवाळो

हरेहरे नावां कुंज लगास्यूँ
बीचाबीचा बारी
साँवरिया रो दरसन पास्यूँ
पहन कसंबी सारी

आधा रात प्रभु दरसन दीस्यूँ
जमनाजी रे तीरा
मीरा रे प्रभु गिरिधर नागर
हिवड़ो घणो अधीरा

Make me Your maid,
Little Lad, make me Your maid.

I'll tend Your plants daily,
Wake to see Your image holy.
I'll sing Your praises,
In Brindavan's green alley.

Your glimpse is my gain,
Thoughts of You, my wage,
Devotion is the estate,
I yearned for ages.

Peacock feather in His crown,
A floral string, neck around,
In Brindavan, He leads the cows,
To graze, as His flute resounds.

I'll grow a green garden,
With bowers of berry,
I'll worship my beloved,
In a saffron sari.

At midnight, O Master,
Come by the river,
Meera's heart is more than eager,
To meet her melodious lover.

Bird-Song

पपइया रे
पिव की बाणि ना बोल

सुणि पावेली बिरहाणी रे
थारो राखेली पाँख मरोड़

चोंच कटाऊँ पपइया
उपरी कालार लूण
पीव मेरा मैं पीव की रे
तू पीव काहे सू कूण

थारा शबद सुहावणारी
जो पिव मिल्या आज
चोंच मढ़ाऊँ थारी सोवनी रे
तू मेरो सिरताज

प्रीतम को पतियाँ लिखूँ
कौवा तू ले जाई
प्रीतमजी सो यूँ कहे रे
थारी बिरहन धान न खाई

मीरा दासी व्याकुली रे
पिवपिव करत बिहाई
बेगी मिलो प्रभु अंतरयामी
तुम बिन रह्यो ना जाई

Hush birdie!
My lover's lines, don't you sing.

Lest the lovelorn listen,
I'll twist your wing.

I'll clip your beak,
And rub salt in,
He's mine, I'm His,
His tune, why do you sing?

I'd call you sweet,
If Him you bring,
I'll gild your beak,
My jay darling.

Take dear dove,
My letter of love.
Tell my beloved,
That His girl is fasting.

Meera, the maid,
Chants Your name,
It's time You came,
Hurry, O Mystic King,
Your absence is killing.

Sleepless

रमैय्या बिन नीन्द ना आवे

नीन्द ना आवे बिरहा सतावे
प्रेमरी आंच दुळावे

बिन पिया ज्योत मंदिर अंधियारो
दीपक दाय ना आवे

पिया बिन मेरी सेज अलूणी
जागत रैन बिहावे पिया कब आवे

दादुर मोर पपीहा बोले
कोयल सबद सुणावे
घुमट घटा उलर होई आई
दामिनी दमक डरावे
नैणा झर लावे

कहा करूँ कित जाऊँ मोरी सजनी
बैदन कूंण बुलावे
बिरह नागण मोरी काया डसे है
लहर-लहर जीव जावे
जडी घसी लावे

को है सखी सहेली सजणी
पियांकू आन मिलावे
मीरा को प्रभु कब रे मिलोगां
मनमोहन मोहि भावे
कबे हंसकर बतलावे

Without You dearest, I'm sleepless.

Sleep taunts, separation haunts,
As I burn loveless.

The temple is dark, sans love's flame,
And the lamp useless.

I toss all night on my bed, depressed,
Come soon love, I'm all stressed.

Bird-song rings,
The koel sings,
Thunder scares,
Lightning strikes,
Eyes rain tears, ceaseless.

Buddy, I'm lost, clueless,
No doctor in sight.
Separation pangs, sting like fangs,
Pound a herbal paste,
I'm in deep distress.

Oh my pal, my buddy, my friend,
Bring home my beloved,
Meera awaits her Master,
Oh, I love the Charmer,
When will You smile and bless?

J. R. SHARMA

The Quirks of Fate

संतो!
करमकी गति न्यारी संतो!

बड़ेबड़े नयन दिये मिरगन को
बनबन फिरत उघारी

उज्वल वर्ण दीनी बगलन को
कोयल कर दीनी कारी

और नदीपन जल निर्मल कीन्ही
समुंदर कर दिनी खारी

मूरखको तुम राज दियत हो
पंड़ित फिरत भिकारी

मीरा के प्रभु गिरीधर नागर
राजाजी को कौन बिचारी?

O Seeker!
The quirks of fate are queer.

Through large eyes peers the deer,
Yet it roams the forest, in fear.

The shrill-voiced heron looks fair,
The dark koel's song is like nectar.

You gave the river a pure flavour,
The sea You gave salty water.

To the fool, You give sovereign power,
The scholar roams unsung, like a beggar.

The Mighty Cowherd is Meera's lover,
Who cares for the ruler?

BIBLIOGRAPHY

Alston, A.J., *The Devotional Poems of Mirabai,* Motilal Banarsidass, Delhi, 1980.

Bahadur, Krishna P., *The Nature of Mira's Love: Mira Bai and Her Padas,* Munshiram Manoharlal Publishers, New Delhi, 1998.

Bhatnagar, Rajendramohan Dr., Marathi translation, Megha Ambike, *Meera,* Manjul Prakashan, Pune, 2006.

Bhelande, Anjali, *Self Beyond Self,* Bharatiya Vidya Bhavan, New Delhi, 1995.

Bihari, Bankey, *The Story of Meerabai,* Gita Press, Gorakhpur, 2008.

Bly, Robert and Hirshfield Jane, *Mirabai, Ecstatic Poems,* Beacon Press, Boston, 2004.

Chopda, Sudarshan, *Meera Parichay Tatha Rachnaye,* Hind Pocket Books, New Delhi, 2002.

Chopra, Swati, *Women Awakened: Stories of Contemporary Spirituality in India,* HarperCollins Publishers and The India Today group, New Delhi, 2011.

Dalal, Suresh, *Kavyavishesh-Mira,* SNDT University, Mumbai, 1991.

Futehally, Shama, *In the Dark of the Heart: Songs of Meera,* HarperCollins Publishers, New Delhi, 1994.

Gulzar, *Meera,* Radhakrishna Publication, New Delhi, 2004.

Jaffrey, Ali Sardar, *Prem Vaani,* Rajkamal Prakashan, New Delhi, 2004.

Kant, Meera, *Meera, Mukti ki Sadhika,* Publishing Department, Information & Broadcasting Ministry, Government of India, New Delhi, 2002.

Khan, Ajra Dr., *Bhakt Meerabai Vyaktitva-Krutitva ki Prasangikta,* Meera Kala Mandir, Udaipur, 1994.

Nagarkar, Kiran, *Cuckold,* HarperCollins Publishers, New Delhi, 1997.

Osho, *Pad Ghunghroo Bandh,* Rebel Books, Pune, 1978.

Padgaonkar, Mangesh, *Meera,* Mouj Prakashan, Mumbai, 1965.

Sangari, Kumkum, *Mirabai and the Spiritual Economy of Bhakti,* Economic and Political Weekly, New Delhi, 1990.

Schelling, Andrew, *For Love of the Dark One: Songs of Mirabai,* Arizona Hohm Press, Prescott, 1998.

Sethi, V.K., *Mira, The Divine Lover,* Radha Soami Satsang Beas, Punjab, 1979.
Upadhyay, Ramprit, *Meera Padavali,* Sharda Prakashan, Kolkata, 1963.
Vedasevanirata, Venkatanarasimhaiah K.V., *Meerabai,* Maharaja Man Singh Pustak Prakash, Jodhpur, 2005.

Music
Mangeshkar, Lata, *Chala Vahi Des,* HMV Records, 2002.

ACKNOWLEDGEMENTS

Meera and I are grateful to all you wonderful souls for helping me manifest my vision:

Ganesh Ramchandran ji for generously supporting the printing of this book. Padmabhooshan Gulzar ji for your blessings.

Thank you Shri. Mahesh Bhatt for the lovingly written foreword.

Thank you Nutan Asgaokar assisted by Nilesh Kavankar, for designing the book and the new cover. Dr Meenaxi Shivram for editing the book. Harsha Bhatkal and the Popular Prakashan team. Dr Ajit Jaiswal, UK for believing in my Meera path.

The family:

My Late Papa Utsahakumar Bhelande. 'Utsaha' means enthusiasm in Marathi. Papa lived every moment of his life with child-like enthusiasm. Thank you for being my biggest fan. Nalini Bhelande, my mother for being an independent, dignified, cultured and spirited woman.

My illustrious sister Dr Anjali Bhelande who is a saint in her own right. Her integrity, values and commitment to the spiritual path make her a living Meera.

My brilliant brother Hemant Bhelande, for being the world's best, coolest bro 😎. The rest of my family-Sandhya, Mrudula, Jason, Abhijit, Emily, and little Sayli.

Blessings of stalwarts, spiritual souls and seniors:

Pujya Swami Chidanand Saraswati, Parmarth Ashram, Rishikesh.

Padmashri Anup Jalota ji. Padmashri Suresh Wadkarji, Late Ravindra Jain ji.

Padmabhooshan Dr Ramakant Panda, Padmashri Pt. Hridaynath Mangeshkar, Padmashri Vyjayanthimala, Shri Vidhu Vinod Chopra, Late Vir Chopra ji.

Shri.Sudarshan Lal Sharmaji,Yogiraj Sarkar Godariwale, Hathras.

Pujya Rakeshbhai,Dharampur, BK Shivaniji. Late Dada Gavand ji.

Shri.Rajiv Kapur ji,Yogi Amarnath ji, Villy Doctorji, Shri. Ajeet Sharanagatji.

Smt Kiran Kheruka ji. Shri.Pradeep Goel ji. Late Leeladevi Somani ji.

Shri Manu Srivastav. Shri Rakesh Asthana. Shri Amit Narang. Shri Ashish Shelar.

Nilesh Moharir for composing 'Radiant Ruby'. Bunkim, Chirag Panchal for the other songs in the album. Padmashri Kailash Kher for co-singing 'Meera danced'.

Friends and fans of Meera & Me:

Dev and Purvi Raman, Sankalp Meshram, Deepak Loyalka, Nidhi Grover, Krishnakant Bajpai, Jasmine Majithia, Shiva Vishwanathan, Bina Shah, Mahesh Kutty, Milind Savey, Baba Jamsandekar, Divyesh Turakhia, Vivek-Harsh Bhagwatkar, Late Narendra Doshi, Sanjay Chhel, Prashant Thackeray, Kishor Amrutkar,Rohini Gandhi, Sanjeev Parekh, Sapna Kar, Ami Virani,Vivek Prakash, Neha Mehta, Vasudha Kothari, Praveen Kumar Singh, Kalpesh Khokhani, Mahek Mane, Late Vinayak Rane, Rupesh Rane, Chirag Panchal, Mohit Shastry, Niranjan Jamkhedkar, Kavarmeet Ghai, Devesh-Sangeeta Gupta, Margaret Joseph, Padmaja-Ramaswamy, Shailatai-Late Ashok Sangoli, Dr Shruti-Late Dr. Anil Sharma, Dr Sanjay-Seema Sharma, Poornima Choksi, Sanjay Mudnaney, Ashank Desai, Prakash Zaveri, Late Deepak Kanegaokar, Shailendra Tiwari, Rohit-Dipti Shah, Aditya Somani, Shatayu-Usha Desai, Late Ashokbhai, Anil Lodhaji, Jay Sharma, Shaila and Satish Jain, Kamal Samodiya, Sandesh Shandilya, Mukesh Sharma, Neena Kothari, Dr Veenu Dhamija, Late Dr Pramod Niphadkar, Namita Jain, Dr. Coomi Vevaina, Dr. Varsha Shirgaonkar, Kunal Kaushal, Ashutosh Kadel, Smt. Rekha Sathe-Joshi,Kshama Daftary,10C girls, Pooja Mohite, Late Manohar Chavan, Vinodiniaunty, Ghodke-kaka, Om-mama, Late Mina aunty, Vaijutai, Vinita, Mohit Roy Sharma.

My overseas friends parivar:

Kishore and Surekha Srinivas, Nitin Talsania,Veena Gandhi, Tushar Manek, Darshna Bhatt, Shailja and Subhash Dhar, Dr Vijay and Ranjna Chhabra, Late Nareshbhai Shah, Hemant Shah, Sanjna and Sayyam Bagade, Madhav-Smita Karhade,Sanjeev Howard, Mehul Kamdar, Gajesh Dhariwal, Sonali Chandorkar, Pratibha Goel, Apoorv Shah, Ameet Mehta.

Students: Sharanya Saxena, Soumya Bagade, Arushi Majumdar, Trisha Krishnan, Mayuka.

All my well-wishers whose names I may have inadvertently missed. Thank you for being there for me. Meera, you all and I are connected 'janam janam se!'

ABOUT THE AUTHOR

The name Sanjeevani means one who gives life. In the *Ramayana*, Lord Hanuman brings the *'Sanjeevani buti'*, a medicinal herb to revive the unconscious Laxmanji. Singer Sanjeevani Bhelande has lived up to her name. When she sings, she breathes life into song after song.

Sanjeevani won the first season of the TV contest 'Saregama. Renowned Music Director Khayyam saheb awarded her the first prize after which Filmmaker Vidhu Vinod Chopra chose her to sing 5 songs of his film *Kareeb*. Her song *'Chorichori jab nazrein mili'* won her the best playback singer Ashirward award in 1999. *'Churalo na dil mera sanam'* was nominated for the Filmfare and Screen awards. Her songs *'Nikamma kiya iss dilne'* from the film *'Kya dilne kaha','Yara rub russ janede'* [Film *Socha na tha*], *'Makhmali yeh Badan"*[film Road] and *'Uljhanonko de diya'* [*Rules- Pyar ka superhit formula*], *Chidiya tu hoti (Nayak)* are chartbusters.

Sanjeevani has performed in more than 2000 live concerts worldwide. She mesmerises her listeners with her soulful *sur*, her resonant voice and graceful presence. Her listeners love the stylistic analysis that she gives into the music and poetry of each song. She is also a much sought after Music Guru.

Sanjeevani has made her foray into music direction and writing lyrics. She has more than a 100 original spiritual tracks to her credit. Her *Laxmiji aarti* has 50 million hits.

Sanjeevani won the Best Music Jury award at the 7th Mumbai Shorts International Film Festival 2018, Best Music Direction award 2019 at the International Film Festival MP for her song from the film *'Bhalobashar Jonye'*. She won the CLEF award for best music composer across all genres and one as best vocalist (Hindustani classical) for her fusion song *'Na daaro rung'* from the album 'Raag in a song'. Her Jain albums include *Jinvani ki Dor and Darshanam Paapnashanam,* an album of Rajasthani songs called *'Gangour'*. She has translated and sung in English the Marathi poems of Saint Tukaram and Samarth Ramdas Swami.

Sanjeevani has sung playback in 14 Indian languages and has sung more than a 100 Nepali songs. Her videos on her YouTube channel have multi-million views. Sanjeevani has trained in Indian Classical music for 40 years by stalwarts like Late. Pandit Dinkar Kaikini, Smt. Shashikala Kaikini, Late Pandit Feroze Dastur and Dr Sandhya Kathavate. She continues her riyaz with Pandit Sudheendra Bhaumik. She holds a degree in Music (Sangeet Visharad), a Master's degree in Commerce and a diploma each in Mass Communication and Film Production. Sanjeevani is trained in Kathak by Reetu Panwar and Odissi dance by Shubhda Varadkar ji. Sanjeevani has founded a Charitable Trust 'Meera & Me' that supports the girl child and classical artists. Her interests include Yoga and gardening.

https://youtu.be/KEiPh-69Apc